The Returning Sky

PETER ROBINSON

Shearsman Books

First published in the United Kingdom in 2012 by
Shearsman Books
50 Westons Hill Drive, Emersons Green
Bristol BS16 7DF

Shearsman Books Ltd Registered Office
43 Broomfield Road, 2nd Floor, Chelmsford, Essex CM1 1SY
(this address not for correspondence)

www.shearsman.com

ISBN 978-1-84861-186-3

Acknowledgements

Most of these poems, or their earlier versions, have appeared in the following print and electronic journals: *Agenda*, *Blackbox Manifold*, *Boomslang*, *The Bow-Wow Shop*, *Cortland Review*, *The Dark Horse*, *Earls Court*, *English*, *Fulcrum*, *Jacket*, *The London Magazine*, *Notre Dame Review*, *Nth Position*, *Poetry Ireland Review*, *Poetry Wales*, *The Reader*, *Shearsman*, *Signals*, *Simulacra*, *Stand*, *Stimulus Respond*, *Tengen*, *Times Literary Supplement*, *Use of English* and *The Warwick Review*.

Several of these poems appeared in four *University of Reading Creative Arts Anthologies* (2008 to 2011). 'Huntley & Palmers', 'Ode to Debt', and 'Graffiti Service' were published with illustrative graphics in the instant collaborative anthology *Fresh Graffiti* (Two Rivers Press, 2008). 'Ekphrastic Marriage' appeared as a limited edition of that name with three artworks by Andrew McDonald from Pine Wave Press in February 2009. 'Cemetery Junction' was also included in *Proceedings of the Conference on Luigi Meneghello* ed. Daniela La Penna. 'Huntley & Palmers' also appeared in the Wokingham *Poetry Windows* project in summer 2009. 'Unearned Visuals' was first published in the festschrift *An Unofficial Roy Fisher* (Shearsman Books, 2010). Some of these poems appeared in the limited, signed hardback edition, *English Nettles and Other Reading Poems*, published by Two Rivers Press with illustrations by Sally Castle in spring 2010. 'World Enough' was printed separately with an additional print by the same artist. 'Credit Flow' appeared as the poem for 18 February in the *Alhambra Poetry Calendar* (2011). Others were published in *Reading Poetry: An Anthology* (Two Rivers Press, 2011). 'Costume Drama' was included in *A Mutual Friend: Poems for Charles Dickens* (Two Rivers Press and The English Association, 2012). My grateful thanks go to their various editors and colleagues.

The Returning Sky

CONTENTS

for Ornella, Matilde & Giulia

ONE

Westwood Dusk

At the corner of Wiltshire and Westwood
what looked like a corpse
had collapsed on the sidewalk,
a smear of saliva
expressed from his lips.

Somebody glanced back,
sun setting on the sea
beyond wild thin frontage,
boulevards, palm trees
and a stoplight's countdown.

I stepped off and ran for my life.
That corpse was out cold
but breathing, and nobody
in the least fazed
at him gone west or westward …

With siren still sounding
a paramedic fire truck
drew up at the bus stop,
those people left standing
around as he lay.

Fixed under a sky glow,
Stranger than Fiction
had opened at the Westwood Crest;
I was checking my direction
with best foot forward,
seeing and believing it there in LA.

At the Institute

after Charles Sheeler

He was touching the hard edge where life and art met.
I was gazing at precisionist
cityscapes and furniture …
and just so's I wouldn't forget
there in a stillness like peace
and silence secured at some price
Mr. President himself was defending his own
legacy, his bloody adventure—
he was 'staying the course,' he would 'get the job done,'
a refurbishment worker's too-loud radio
come thoughtlessly from an adjacent room …
and just so's I wouldn't forget
there *The Artist Looks at Nature*
was a painter in his studio
touching the hard edge where life and art met.

30 November 2006

Enigma Variations

1. Noir

But what had I done to deserve
this room's slatted blinds,
its film noir shadows across bed covers?
Thrown back on myself alone,
nothing much left by way of resources,
I was stood stark staring awake
with only curiosity
to save me from implosion.

2. At the Reading

Now when somebody volunteered a question
I was certain I'd seen him before
and started as if … but couldn't have done …

Yes, that was the day's metaphysical picture:
invited to defend what you know
by the spitting image of a Giorgio de Chirico.

3. Night Watch

Christmas tree decked out on the thirteenth floor,
there's nobody in or, no, a woman home alone,
who sees me at this hotel window—
gone like a Bathsheba with her mobile phone.

Back at the glass, now, she closes drapes on snow
turning to sleet down North Michigan Avenue
as it gusts across a lit storefront
devoted to Rembrandt born four-hundred years ago.

South Shore Line

Randolph

Somewhere still in earshot at millennium station,
granddad, you'd never have believed I got this far
dragging a silver case through the slushy snow
melted to curb pools on North Michigan Avenue.

But what with the family's fear of missing trains,
I'd reached here, as it happened, soon enough
to fetch my glasses from that left hotel room
and still catch the earliest service to South Bend.

Roosevelt

Snow blown in off the lake last night had whirled
around each streetlamp, while a solitary car
would gingerly be steering its soft-sprung way ...

Trestles thrown across this whiteness gone by,
I stare back at them as if from your eyes
through misted carriage windows and soft snow.

Kensington

Down through the back of your memory that panic
over train-times must have been a fear of losing jobs,
it struck me, as our two cars rolled past freight yards,
house yards, factory walls and the housing projects.

And that's how we'd left south central Chicago,
its automobiles down on their suspensions
and streets with NO ENTRY signs all along the way
—as if tempting passersby even, well, to try.

Gary Metro

Further, more snow flurries turning to thin rain,
WELCOME TO GARY it spelt out on the town hall,
but still your familiar rust-belt squalor
couldn't make me feel any more at home.

By painted clapboard houses ran our corrugated train,
screen doors tacked up with cards that read FOR SALE
(sub-prime, though I didn't know the term,
and, granddad, they so weren't going to be sold).

Hudson Lake

Money growing tighter, as it had in your hey-day,
where I even less belong, no one seemed to belong
and south the Saint Joe river bends—

granddad, I had got this far … where farmers have a tall silo
and at gateless crossings, our train had to slow …
and the engineer made his lonesome horn blow.

Enigmas of Departure

for John Matthias

It was while I walked out to the plane
readied on an apron at Giuseppe Verdi airport,
hair raised by the breeze
and a few spots of rain
spattering the tarmac,
across its spaces came a sense
of release in roaring silence
before being cabined, cribbed, confined …
And while I walked out from the gate
it caught me once again
as at South Bend, Michiana,
since we also had to wait
while our O'Hare plane arrived,
and the Michiana field
hazes off equally in a great plain …
Not that much wanting to go or to stay
but exposed in their flatness,
what I would fleetingly feel
from another winter's journey in the vastness
was an isolate air around frame houses
in yards out beyond wide sidewalks and a green
expanse, right, then a grey one
as we were cleared for take-off and were gone
to put yet more distance between.

Peripheral Visions

Glimpsing a stretch of dawn skyline
revealed by raw spaces between
the lopped poplar trunks,
pillars of a screened villa's drive
I turn and in the window
(like a hinged mirror) catch sight of you …
Although a perpetual hum
of trucks on the ring-road reaches my ear,
we can see them now
as they rev out through our *periferia*.

Yet more, as I've caught my reflection
and yours reappears in the glass
where Daphne's wild arms used to wave,
I see it's like this any time
we arrive from elsewhere and are lost
by slip road, lorry park, by-pass:
the signs have too much, or no sense at all,
like an eyeful of how things appear
when we're not used to them …

Yet more, as its reflection
glimmers in a rear-view mirror,
I see it's like this any time
we arrive from elsewhere, foxed
by a new gyratory system
or half-erected towers and cranes;
the town's a rash of roundabouts—
and we'll be lost once more
among growth rings, ripe stains
of year after year after year.

Huntley & Palmers

1

Then that tightening in the chest
and tear-duct, like a taste
of whatever it might be,
comes with the looked-at brick façade
seen on a canal bank walk
but in so much perspective,
with the strollers' voices
heard as if by alien ears
(ones too full of other views,
views, reverses and reversals)
as if from somewhere else.

2

That taste could be digestive biscuit.
A sudden scent of wood smoke
rises across locked, sluggish water
where a drowned white bicycle
seems to float up from the depths.
Further, assailed by all this flooding
laburnum, ivy, rape field yellow,
wisteria that thrives in the good spring
weather, there's a memory of pain,
of pain, though not of its sensation—
no, no, I wouldn't be without it,
looking at what's left, and gone.

Whiteknights Park

Pigeons poised at grey pinnacles
struck by summer sunlight
ruffle feathers like ghosts in stone.
A squirrel darts along black fence-work,
pauses on some vertical bark;
it warily eyes an ivy-covered
convenient escape route …
Just think we might be home to stay!
Still, they keep their station.

Then magpies soar up to survey
traces of late revelries,
a taxi waiting by the flagstaff
for somebody's getaway;
or it's an African parakeet
flies over coverts, foliage tremors,
across this habitat-retreat
with likelihood of a brimful lake
and Human Resources pondering dilemmas.

What differences a day could make!
That idyll had one student girl
reading, back against a tree,
eras gone, or just last night;
its silver-birch bark, mottled shade,
defined for us an out-of-term
late afternoon when, under them—
a part of her philosophy—
swan broods had got it made.

165 King's Road

Equivocal days: the return of weather
like a further dice throw
takes us unawares;
neither one thing nor another,
the days dawn, slowly go
with a shopping list of skies, chores, and new cares.

Disorientated as ever
seeing as we're back,
back from our travels in Southern or in Eastern climes,
I'm staring at a cream façade
puzzled as to whether
this is the address Rimbaud gave in *The Times*.

Showers, sunbursts, deep leaf shadows
meet the passing hours
and not only, everything shrieks at me—
early May sunlight on swollen gooseberries,
tentacles of fronds vertiginously
swaying in a breeze.

What with graffiti rashes, it's like being in a daze
though I'm under no illusions
about skies' capricious changes, elongated afternoons
and drawn-out evenings,
extraordinary garden choruses
where a late bird sings.

Now swans, their cygnets, ducks, all types of pigeons
touch Kennet banks or Thames
and notwithstanding your attainments,

whatever, your good references,
I'm under no illusions.
It's as if some wheel of fortune had come round.

Pension Scheme

'Mrs. Cheveley: "Even you are not rich enough,
Sir Robert, to buy back your past. No man is."'
Oscar Wilde, *An Ideal Husband*

i.m. Siobhán Kilfeather

Let the dead borrow our eyes
beside a canal bank walk as swans
with cygnet balls of fluff beside them
float on their reflections—

for when familiar faces come
and take us unawares,
bringing bitter news
of one who won't find out what happens
in her family soap-operas,
you see, a gap appears
in which two almost strangers
precariously perched on high stools of a pub
sip swift halves ruminating on
having kids of their own
before baby-sitting in a Dublin suburb …

but now familiar faces come
and take us unawares,
I'm summing up our losses
with the spiders' handiwork, quotations, house repairs;
you see, because they're so expensive,
we can never buy back the years.

Graffiti Service

The aerosol boys have been at it again
making signature loops and swirls,
soccer boasts, names of girls
on stone, glass, concrete, pebble-dash house-front …
You said I should take them, citing me,
as welcomes: we'd gone past a substation door
decked out in swathes of graffiti.
So I daub the town with words once more.
But, today, council workers are out on their round
depersonalizing public space
with industrial spray-gun, solvent and paint—
like an artist preparing a ground.

Like a Foreign Country

That much would have to be explained:
how cloud-roofs at dawn
were burned off by a July sun
and showers washed out washing day,
how identity theft protection
or laundry would get done
when there was the tax disc to display.

It was time, time to cultivate our garden
where blades of whitened grass
hid creatures still alive
beneath their mossy stone,
or in a creosoted shed
with ivy bursting through its boards—
still lives of paint cans, and so on.

That much had been left behind.
Cloud-diffused sunlight would soothe
my jangled nerves. You'd find
it was like our daughter's school report:
me too, I'm happy as can be
expected, coping well
with moving ... in a foreign country.

Days gone, terraces, terra incognita,
were like our faces redefined
at a bathroom mirror when it's cleaned;
for time had taken its advantage
over us, the gained
and lost perspectives realigned.
That much would have to be explained.

In the Playground

Dawn comes, bright as a button
hanging by a thread
on the coat front of a waif-faced girl
who crosses the playground at my daughter's school
with the look of one I might have known
when we were ten years old.

I see her knees, blue from the swimming pool,
straggled blonde hair, quick eyes
of a bird in flight above an airport runway;
but like at ten years old
they glance off mine with that look of defiant
indifferent daylight, as I might have known.

Credit Rating

Twilight, with a greenish glow,
near journey's end, you tell me
those pale shapes in darkness,
they're a cemetery … but no,
through the hazy screen I see
or, better, I hazard a guess
that rather than a cemetery
it's an estate agent's window.

Personal Credit

'a blank, my lord'
Twelfth Night

Rain in the small hours, yet more rain
falls on roof and misted glass,
on the floor of a half-woken mind …
Likewise, to relish the scenery,
I dawdle on errands and try
my best to borrow colouring
from gasholders, flood pools, lemon verbena,
to lend them something of a mind;
it's a mind distracted by
a few white clouds, quite still
in turquoise over rooflines,
clouds sun-struck as me
by Personal Credit premises,
not a sign of life inside
under this summery sky.

Mirrored in the surface run-off,
past sleeping policemen and double-parked cars,
I lend a mind caught in the wars
of nerves set going by today's cold calls.
They're offers to let us pay back our way.
Although we have no history,
everyone wants to confirm our postcode.
Likewise, on its rain-greased road,
we're reflected in the flood
of dead cats, floated furnishings,
the flashed-back pasts, denied facts, things,
insurance claims and more.

Ode to Debt

'All progress is based upon the universal innate desire
on the part of every organism to live beyond its means.'
Samuel Butler

1

Consulting the Oracle one Saturday
in a mid-afternoon's mayhem,
lads with their edgy energy
are jostling pensioners, some
emboldened to scold them, who get
an earful for their pains ...

2

Hordes are pouring along the gauntlet
of arcade emporia filled
with promise to be bought with promises—
and this is the rock on which we build.
Banks and building societies
have queues outside their doors.

3

We're in them like panicked investors
who've done their getting and spending elsewhere:
so lenders just won't trust us.
Away too long, we're advised to get
a history, a rating that tells
how we've coped with the daylight of debt.

4

So consulting the Oracle one Saturday
we flow with the crowd, as flow we must,
into that double-edged ledger,
the future, whose sibylline leaves
have spelt in small print just days
when the large sums will come out, I trust.

Double Portrait

after Frans Hals

So there we are: by a garden wall's
re-pointed summer shade,
by vines encircling tree trunks, ivy
clinging to its brick
or trailed across some mildewed concrete;
thistles, spilled pots, other symbols
do their best to place us
where heart-shaped leaves lie thick, entwined,
like living necklaces.

Tendrils knocking at a window
insistently had wormed on through
gaps between aperture and frame.
Still, the blocked light came;
and though we love leaf-shadow thrown
across a bathroom floor,
in your heart of hearts you know
that this infesting mass of creeper,
it will have to go.

Far language seeps from crevices
in an August's holding truce:
the girls are playful somewhere near,
speaking other tongues.
A butterfly with red-flecked wings
rises from composted grass
beside them; only they don't notice,
lost in art works, making things,
don't see it disappear

across the distance, somewhere other,
to where a villa's peacocks
patrolling box hedge arch their necks,
shriek imprecations at a sky
with dusk tints, warmer cloud,
like choking, being sick. Your mother
mimics them alarmingly,
but the family's drawn together—
don't ask me how, or why.

So there we are: a married couple
pausing in our day
to laugh out loud at contradiction,
those emblems of it on display;
and farther are the ancestors
like staffage, nymphs and shepherds
sweating through a checkered past.
They're figured down to us as myth,
love, in so many words.

A Little Exercise

'All in the golden afternoon
Full leisurely we glide …'
  Alice in Wonderland

'They hadn't gone much farther before
the blade of one of the oars got fast in
the water and *wouldn't* come out …'
  Through the Looking Glass

Down, down in the river meadows,
beyond a long oak drive
with its contested histories
that they'll have witnessed and the towpath's
interrupted shadows,
we take our time about it; we arrive
where boathouses are set back from the brink,
activities get under way,
the scullers bearing shells above their heads
will float themselves out on the current,
and it makes you think.

This early on the river, now, an oarsman
backs into his morning while
a bike-rider with megaphone
is bellowing words, words of advice
at the viewless stylist
who makes you think he's anyone
effortfully distancing a past
of dowdy summers, overblown
ambitions, yes, as we glide on
by weeping willows with their ghosts
of *sfumatura* leaves …

Then from a sticky, shade-mottled day
here come its dark towers
silhouetted against late afternoon sky;
and the day, as done by Seurat,
sees me moving like a fish back in water.
Later, through grass voices rise.
They're language students' macaronics
unmixed before, recalling
consonant clusters from remote skies
and, haunted by them, I catch snatches
of a future in quotation.

That squirrel's gnawing at a pizza,
holding it in small front paws.
The coaches call out jargon to their scullers.
Figures pause on famous bridges
hearing jazz or chatter borne
by pleasure steamers, flat-iron cruisers ...
You can't pull and give advice at the one time:
to left or right our two girls guide me
backing, with uncertainty,
on a zigzag course towards
futures made of words.

Across the landscapes with dead dons
I'm looking out for further clues,
for traces of what happens
when everywhere's soured by quarrels, civil wars.
Conflicted signs of histories
have turned from us, give little away.
Silence fills the avenues.
Then it's like they're oblivious,
have had enough of crowds like ours
gone into deepening shadows
under the dumb oak trees.

Recovered Memory

for Adam and Jane Clarke-Williams

1

Geese below a gasholder
slide through spangles of the sun's
autumnal glints on wavelets;
they compete with swans for crumbs,

and ducks steer round a rusted cage
where, look, a shopping trolley
lies in shallows at the conflux
of the Kennet and the Thames.

Here the painted barges come,
weekend water-folk at their tillers,
past cygnet, swan, or duck flotillas
under Brunel's bridge.

Back to what can't be got round,
I come out from my reverie
and find a pair of splashing coots
feud like rival poets.

They nut each other with their beaks.
Circling, a third bird squawks—
the object or cause of it all?
Or she's their referee ...

2

Now look at that leafless blasted oak—
a Laocöon ... and I awake

to find myself in Hampshire
on a fresh, autumnal day
hearing word from familiar friends
up here on the Ridgeway.

Later, they point out mountain ash
by black wrought-iron railings,
as if this were all taking place
only to jog a memory;
and they tell me, among other things,
it's also called the rowan tree.

3

As one home from the near half-dead
might wonder had he visited
this place in a previous life,
bombarded with cow parsley scents

you drift by city gates above
places for meeting another lost love,
come back with cut grass,
fireworks, and the plaster dust …

Then passing fast, I saw
a badger with its four paws
lifted in the air
like it was playing possum.

Road-killed, not culled, it bore
that stricken resemblance
to yet another of our present,
ill-remembered wars.

4

Dandelion clock transparencies
are flecked with wild poppies.
Their petals flap like butterfly wings,
red admirals in a breeze.

Released into the last of sun,
shadows of my daughters
beneath election hoardings
cross through littered, civic lawn.

Wildings form a bonsai forest
of pines sprung up where two walls meet,
catching wind-blown seed
to start this latest generation.

5

Not many days after our return
you rushed out shouting 'Via! Via!'
at that magpie in the branches
of a silver birch tree.

More slowly off my haunches,
I was there in time to see
it grudgingly flap through the darkness
on its white-flashed wings.

'Dad, is there anywhere *you* feel's home?'
asked my younger daughter
just a day or two later
on her way from school.

So when I glimpse a magpie
settled in the sink-hole
of that green cast-iron fountain,
it seems best leave it be.

6

Like an interrupted programme:
we found monkey-puzzle-tree
saplings in their wired cages
on grounds of a National Trust property—

as if this were a crash from
some freak electric storm
or power out, and data
looked lost only to flash back later;

encoded deep, a memory of pain,
it comes with fallen apples
arranged around a well-head
glistening in the rain.

7

No, all losses aren't restored
by sheaves of sunlit ivy
to deck a harvest festival
along the brick-faced cutting wall,

squirrels scouting for their store,
but made up for, God knows;
and I'm grateful for small mercies
as the daylight goes—

when on the lower reaches
with all this world before us,
in the shadow of St Paul's
sun-flared through estuary air,

there's a father and his child
beachcombing by the waterside,
plaits and tangles in her hair
reported on the tide—

yes, made up for, believe you me,
by glimpsed roofs on a far shore,
therefore in the offing glow
of recovered memory.

Cemetery Junction

'it was like beginning life again, with some of
the vividness that we have in childhood. Things
seemed absurdly vivid and significant.'
   Luigi Meneghello, *La materia di Reading*

Cemetery Junction, under the rain …
its entrance, death's triumphal arch,
stands out against the sky's plain grey
and dirtied life in ephemeral floods
of traffic choosing east or south-east
separates around fume-smutted sandstone.
That neo-classical gatehouse bars
buses and cars from the choice of straight on:
it's imposing, in its way.

Today, though, in a graveyard mood
and strolling down its avenues
as haze hesitates at the tops of yews
or cedars, you can pause
with grass grown waist-high at a slant
bleared angel, cross, a tombstone.

It's got little to do with self-preservation,
this epitaph hunt from stone to stone;
even worn weather-smutched words go on
regardless, without us, traffic noise
dividing beyond ivied patches of wall;
and nor will ignored kids substitute for
immortality: growing apart, you remain
a student of the graveyard school
at Cemetery Junction under the rain.

To the Quick

1

Quick was a word troubled me that much
on Sundays when a kid at church.
My father, in his surplice, said:
'and He shall come to judge both the quick and the dead.'

2

Someone explained it meant: *the living.*
I'll have thought to keep moving
was how we avoid such a fate
when mum said, 'Quick, quick, or you're going to be late!'

3

But, now it's a Sunday, what distresses
are gust-beaten grasses
and stubborn leaves crinkled from autumn
clinging through that quickness with the chill still to come.

Graveyard Life

'there are no countries in the world less known
by the British than these selfsame British Islands'
George Borrow

for Tom Phillips

Glimpses of the Muntjac deer
in cemetery undergrowth
are rubbed out by what place-names hint,
where signposts point
around its arch of quiet life
with cedar, willow, privet, yew …

The cemetery, needless to say, a dead-end,
its far brick wall
backs on terrace house-backs,
the devil in all their detail—
a cat shooed off an outhouse roof,
cascading frozen ivy …

But who would have guessed that here,
where criminals were interred
beyond town limits and a crossroads gibbet,
idling one afternoon
we'd meet a safari photographer
with barrel lens and tripod
in search of the sacred or scared?

Who would have guessed that Muntjac deer
surviving by carved angels
(like creatures off old land mass edges)
would point to one more great unknown
under my nose, in this hemisphere?

World Enough

Such as it is, imagine this
sunset centuries ago,
guess what brick courses
saw by way of costume drama
in twilight whether anyone
was watching it or no.

Such as it is, reality
slips past on a warehouse
without the slightest emphasis,
thrives if it fail to become
yet one more news item—
hoarfrost, a whisper, or kiss.

Such as it is, and everywhere,
it comes at us sideways
from bits of grey sky
as when a bureaucrat asked me
where did I plan to be buried?
I wasn't planning to die.

TWO

Clear as Daylight

'*The dancers, faces oblivious & grave,—*
testing testing
the dancers face oblivion and the grave.'
        Geoffrey Hill,
        'After Reading *Children of Albion* (1969)'

Reading in an early dawn—
you're distracted glancing over
edges of slim volume pages
and words, too fathomable words
cross patios, backyards,
outliving children of Albion
who face death now, as best they can,
while the first birds sing.

To identify with where we live
I read us into every thing,
like the cut of some salt-crusted brickwork …
though, try as I might,
dripping tap and leaky cistern
gall me to the quick,
like one swan biting at another's neck—
as if we'd never learn.

But even the things I'm reading
strayed among wild rhubarb
are moving over surfaces
of cloud types, sun- and storm-light,
that heat has flaked to pieces
and they're sublimed, resentment-free,
like purgatories in others' verses,
to skies filled with activity.

Owning the Problem

'and it is but grief to have come home
if one cannot return to oneself.'
F. H. Bradley

Lath-ceilings down, through cracks
in the landing floorboards
and hall's revealed rafters
there come light-chinks from below;
it's like that filmic nightmare
in which I tread, precarious,
on a tenement stair.

The broken light-chinks underline
a powder of blown plaster dust.
We're covered in it, see
how even soiled laundry
migrates from room to room
in this unfixed home
or stays put, as it must.

       *

They put me in mind of emergency floor
lighting or gleams at the end
of a tunnel and stripped bedroom door
forming an exit before me.

Down fracture lines, the light-chinks lead
back where we begin again;
and I feel my way over joists through pitch darkness
as if above the Siberian plain …

       *

So much that had to be postponed
returns with the light-chinks in your eye
it's like, despite severe headwind,
past promise is renewed while we try,
heaven knows, to strike the note
of home (or get tradesmen to quote).

Untidy Bedroom

for Matty & Giulia

Uncurtained sill clutter, cactus, clothes,
here a nightlight for our girls,
an amber street-lamp has been hung
like one of those luminous globes.

Slowed by mini-roundabouts,
headlamps of stray cars
track over bedroom interiors
a-flicker with sudden doubts.

                    *

Now years' distances compact
in our flooded drain pools,
their glassed surfaces cracked
by late passing souls.

Across picture frames the beams track.
Higgledy-piggledy shadows try
to mitigate that fact
in the blues from our latest sky.

                    *

But then this upstairs corridor
(a poster-ed door ajar
above its fit of polished floorboards)
is filled with music for the young.

It holds me, holds me still,
her lyric on forsaking, song
of disappointed love
and she just twelve years old.

*

'Crying in progress' was the phrase
scrawled beside an entrance
to that daughter's private space,
and I couldn't not think

of flood-covered games fields, surfaces
rippling to a marooned pavilion,
all the more mess outside
beyond us, barred by that brink.

*

Chaotic sunset, sewage, there's this
stretch of blazed flood waters
drowning rail beds, family cars—
and a young girl's sense of justice,

her urge to have them all decried,
are summed up in that phrase
about some stuff which wasn't fair
and not just at the end of those days.

120 Addington Road

Now, mother, with your need to know
we lead you past the fuchsias
down our patch of garden; now
you're settled in the front room
turning out scales on an upright piano,
two-handed; now you're being shown
the narrow kitchen, its larder store—
built round the year the stock market collapsed,
our house about as old as you are.

Withdrawn, foul weather
at the glass once more,
you see we're thrown together
in our tight corner
behind a flaked, black-painted door ...

and, mother, with your need to know,
now when you picture this inter-war
semi, sense its compact ground plan
imprinted from the precipitous stairs
to where new copper piping leads;
now when you rehearse your prayers
imagining how each room succeeds
room; now when you lie down to sleep,
mother, remember us, mum, if you can.

Reading Gaol

'the salesman … knows nothing of what he is selling
save that he is charging a great deal too much for it.'
            Oscar Wilde, 'House Decoration'

Reading gaol from Reading town
(*Homebase*, to be precise)
has weed-tufts sprouted from a chimney pot,
one crenellated central tower
with apertures barred, still rising above
sheer, featureless, brutist walls.

There's a sunset blazed across glass façade
where we go to cost soft furnishings,
to match non-toxic paints.

From a customer car-park, Reading gaol
imposes high above the flow
of rush-hour traffic round a roundabout;
so that's where he would learn the price
of everything there was to pay …

Receipts checked in a bloodstained dusk,
the glint of its lit windows
and perimeter arc-lights about the new wing,
by Reading gaol, I see
where if you killed the thing you love
you'd die in earnest, that's no jest;
where, his social credit spent,
they would kill the thing they hate
with the power of the State
and, really, a trial cannot end like a play.

Ekphrastic Marriage

for Peter Swaab and Andrew McDonald

1

Slants of companionate sun
are coming to the rescue
across slim volume spines, disks, pictures.
They touch each scratch and scar.
A street scene from an upstairs window,
one grandly battered car
parked beside the yellow door,
is framed too as you draw back curtains.
The kitchen sink from last night's party,
banter sounding until late,
bares remnants of your taken pains.
Slow silence now, first daylight
picks across a crusted palette,
leaves the pots and pans to do …
Found like an ekphrastic marriage,
love lies in its element
and home is where the paintings are.

2

More, when the *sposa bagnata*
had been rained on enough to bring luck,
we were scanning the sky for a change in the weather—
advised to hold off with our speeches
until cloud thinned, as you did.
Then a sun slant broke through orchard trees,
mottling seventeenth-century brick;
it had painted a glitter across Broad water.
Bright in damp air, disturbed wasps from their nest

stung neither host nor guest.
Careless of such identities
as gain definition by attacking another,
that sun's oblique beam touched farthest reaches:
it struck us all, included.

Costume Drama

'his ventures had been utterly reckless'
Charles Dickens, *Little Dorrit*

Under their broad bacchanalian ceiling,
a film company moved in its canopied bed
for the death scene, but of whom?

False shutters were tacked over windows,
a reprobate gentleman dunned for debt.
They had placed tall white candles
by mirrors in that makeshift bedroom
for a theatrical gloom.

They had built themselves a pontoon bridge
to track from the Temple of Venus
across lake water to a stately pleasure dome,
a fictional Venice forbidden us …

Around the lake, stray extras roamed.
Duckweed rafts were shooting a sluice.
It was like the shady bathtub end
of a banker, a banker with annual bonus
—or so I imagined.

West Wycombe Park

Eastern Avenue

'for a vast speculation had fail'd'
Alfred Tennyson

1

As dawn mist climbs where Eastern Avenue's
patched-up tarmac slopes,
two schoolgirls are blurred out and squirrels, I suppose,
past a front lawn's littered landscapes,
leaf-mould smells, signs of night's revelries.
World-stuff brick, its
yo-yo markets,
have value written off in the haze-edged trees.

2

Purplish splotches through more low cloud cover
form a bruised red dawn.
It's like the economists hadn't a clue.
Their boasts echo rat-run
traffic through unprecedented weather
on Eastern Avenue.

3

That figures your reverie's baffled grief,
like a disappointment
in every leaf,
this blustered-down, far-flung, red-tinged to-do,
or else a missed appointment
on Eastern Avenue.

Unearned Visuals

for Roy Fisher

That bungalow protected by Decaux hoardings,
a one-off industrial cottage has
two chimney pots, bayed windows,
the green door in between them
and lemon-daubed brickwork, smutted now;
it blanks me, close up, appears to hide
behind those images.

Its grey net curtains and metal-stud door,
steep roof-slope, lemon brick, what's behind?
I've never seen anyone enter or leave,
just looking, on the way to work.
In gravel pit lodge, as was,
not a thing's astir.

Past crescent shops where trams would turn,
stood forward of the building line
it's hidden from package holiday vistas,
spectacular bank accounts, high definition
pay-as-you-watch-them franchise wars …
weekend supplement pages!

That cottage concealed behind Decaux hoardings
has a yard screened by their dark side.
After working, I think you'll find,
here in the shadow of a bigged-up world,
unearned, though it seems to hide
like rain-smell coming from an overcoat,
the actual imagined.

Otterspool Prom

'O cursed spite'
Hamlet

There's a dazzle of sunlight on the low-tide river
and our far shore
has a silver-grey blur, bright as never, never,
ever before.

You see it's enough to bring tears to the eyes
by silhouetting trees,
winter boughs spidery on mist-like white skies
twitched in a breeze.

But then down the promenade its flyers release
their dragon-tailed kite;
frost on the pitches is shrinking by degrees;

a student's words return, her going 'England's shite!'
and I'm like 'Please
yourself' in sunshine born as if to set it right.

17 February 2008

Gasometers

'Le souvenir vivace et latent d'un été
Déjà mort, déjà loin de moi ...'
    Raymond Roussel, *La Vue*

Seen again from the First Great Western,
'This town's growing on me,' said
the passenger, slowed towards its station,
where two routes converge.

Thick gas pipes snake from underground
to cross the Kennet's course
beside a red-brick rail bridge,
water reflections speckling its arch.

              *

Now the old tank's all but empty,
its structure open to a sky
flecked about with bits of cloud,
a man's head in the framework spaces.

'Politician,' you guessed out loud,
photographed to make his point
above the biscuit factory houses
or boarded up pub windows ...

              *

I liked them too, could see better days
in an avenue's baking roof-tiles,
a loaded pear bough's greens on brick,
grey structures up above the trees;

and all my future hopes, ambition,
to be read in black & white
like an end wall's painted advert
faded, years back, by the sun.

*

To think of them, gasometers,
depressed, lost like this advert
uniquely able to appear,
when light falls from an angle;

of bifurcated time at last
entwined by their faint reek
into a parallel belle époque
materializing from staled air,

*

from sharp-cut shadows, blued
leaves reflective of that sky;
and they call back possibilities,
the summer, say, of '75—

its fugitive touch come to the rescue
in an airy jump-cut series
emerging from the crowd to kiss you,
still here, still alive.

Mortgaged Time

At the calm point of our summer,
I let a soul in torment
fly out through kitchen windows.
An abandoned villa front
had row on row of shutters
dangling by their hinges.
We'd found ourselves among the ruins
of a family's histories.
Sore eyes
took in the cool, quick-flowing waters.

Where a demolition process
was helped by rampant ivy,
tangles of intestines
hung from warehouse roofs;

through their shard-edged windows,
a start of pigeon wings
took flight for open air.
They at least had made their moves.

Everybody knows
we're working off the mortgaged time,
snatching at securities
as it runs fast through cupped fingers.
Paying back the past, a loan
we took out on ourselves,
you hold fast till a touch of breeze
revivifies the evening leaves—
living in hope, love, as the saying goes.

By a Wayside Shrine

Advice is trampled like confetti
around a cash machine;
pilgrim-fashion, lives form a line,
and leaves retire to die.

I'm counting on the issuer
to utter currency, reassure—
graced as it is with signature graffiti
under an untold sky.

Credit Flow

Rescued from a lost afternoon—
I wasn't much company for anyone; but
you drove me out of that aloofness,
not far, to where farm chimneys
shared a sky with flustered trees.

By the flooded gravel pits,
seeing migrant species fly
suddenly in their fancy thousands,
it's as if I needed the assurance
of wigeon, teal, mute swans …

or reassurance of a day,
a wintry dusk like any other
and its chilly wind
threatening one more snow event—
another day been lent to us,
but not to be returned.

18 February 2009

The Visitant

'Bist du ein Engel? fragte das eine Kind.
Ich wollte, ich wär' es, versetzte Mignon.'
        Goethe, *Wilhelm Meisters Lehrjahre*

'You're an angel,' said the young man at our door
as he took a cardboard box from you
and I thought, yes, you are—
but one who has to get out of the house,
who feels the cold perpetually
like Mimi and her gelid hands,
who knows the land where an avenue's trees
with lopped lower branches form
an entrance to the town …

Imagine, though translated far,
how further south in our hemisphere
she'd go to cure a childhood illness
at Monticelli Terme once,
a town among its bar umbrellas
solidified from somnolence, the place
for peace talks, local ones
where only lizards squabble under wrought-iron chairs.

Like a mirage in the heat-stunned plain,
here you are, love, here you are—
a woman formed from sun-struck air
as I picture you, before we met,
under an avenue of shaped plane trees
leading from that spit-sized thermal spa …

'You're an angel,' as the man said at our door.

English Nettles

for Ornella

Blue-black crows flap up the acid yellow
of a rape seed field and, well, now
all these chestnut candelabra
are bringing yet more news from nowhere
as the piled white clouds above us
mute their sun-struck colour.

But what it most brings home, this heat,
in terms of skin and shadows,
bare arms, the warm grass, naked feet
stalking with tanned knees
is a sense from thirty years back
of some possibilities …

Now look at the revelry's aftermaths!
Tuppence coloured mandarins
come waddling over can-strewn grass
as if to tell how less is more
or less all there'll ever be in store
for the likes of us!

Through buttercups, tufted cow parsley,
thistles, stinging nettles, dock,
there you go across wild parkland—
peculiarly coloured by circumstance.

Usage and tones of the local fauna
can't help unsettling, their behaviour
like to get you hence.

But then you grasp the nettles,
pull them up in fistfuls,
as if for recompense.

Love amid the alien settles
on omelettes, soups, odd vegetables;
and, love, you turn that hapless stinging
into sustenance.

Fence Palings

'Es war einmal ein Lattenzaun …'
Christian Morgenstern

Fierce sun strikes my daughter's face
as she turns back to the door
and smiles, smiles, late for school;

then hurtles off around the corner …
It's as if between brick courses,
the cut grass patch's grass blades,
or fence palings' empty spaces
were your possibilities,
ones no architect could steal
nor councillor condemn—

and, again, I'm thinking of
interstices, the front path pebbles',
so many you could never tell
their number, number possibilities,
troubles, homework, love,
as again I'm thinking of
your welfare and farewell.

THREE

Abroad Thoughts

for Bill Manhire

Home I'd come with my own OE.
After lunch after twenty-odd years and more,
you compared me to some non-dead returnee
from a distant war …

We were paused by the statue of Edith Cavell
where I muddled up quotations:
it was 'Patriotism is not enough,' Bill,
not 'the Lord is high above all nations.'

The Returning Sky

Blocked, the drain-flood lake out front
is like a dirty moat now.
Workmen come sucking-up sodden, black leaf-fall;
the surface water seeps away
and there we are, before this house,
with a fresh access of sky.

The neighbour fir trees, opposite,
succumb to saws in daylight
and that's what gives us so much blue
to populate with relatives,
acquaintances or others' loved ones,
last things, the latest cry ...

This season too has done its bit;
gone, our deciduous screens.
Bare branch-shadows on a white house wall
make more intricate vein-work,
and they're added to the flooded gutters'
leaves painted-up with sky.

Now our lately dead are in the air.
An overcast grey-scale dusk's
shot through with thin red cloud streaks;
and, look, they're everywhere
in privet hedges, like a private grief
for the targeted to die.

You incorporate them, part and whole—
synapse, nerve-end, heart brimful,
as any body knows:

it's like death were a white van driver
who had splashed us differently,
indifferently going by.

Life in Glimpses

Like that landscape with its winter hunters,
an occasional pale or an amber
light glints in the outskirts.
I look out before dawn on the first of the year:
white ground, black air
from which the far lights flare.

Then, through thick filigree
of frozen fog along poplar tree
branches, come phosphorous plumes of war;
and evil is done in return
among *memento mori*
of each whited sepulchre.

You trace a dog's, then a pigeon's tracks.
What were nerve-shredding reports
from mortars, petards
(or like, for that matter, champagne corks)
are firecracker remnants
cushioned on a pristine fall of snow.

Later, in bleak-stubborn sunlight
that pristine fall gave way
to dark glints, wetness, crevices
from the day before,
our sorry world's injustices—
surgical cruelties, still another war.

Later yet, a fingernail moon
hung in a start-of-year sky
where we were to glimpse at its fringes
(of a pallid blue with flaky pink,

suddenly more of it now
a whole block's been demolished)
that chilly landscape with winter hunters
setting further challenges
out there, where they burn and freeze once more.

1 January 2009

Shadowy Nobodies

'such shadowy nobodies, as cherub-winged
DEATH ... & simpering PEACE ...'
Samuel Taylor Coleridge

As from a back bedroom window
like living the form of a dream,
a dream dreamed lifetimes or centuries ago,
you imagine yourself in that view
when the abstract threats in person
make themselves felt from beyond its frame.
They push through your deadlines, your daily distraction,
but forget them is all you can do.

Now the more indifferently far they are
the more I can't explain
or justify ordinary domestic tiffs,
our self-consoling griefs
as a daughter's convulsed by the ring-tone
from her importunate phone.

The sun-suffused clouds press on,
pointed at by aerials
and chimney pots in an afternoon sky;
they move above rooftops as burning anguish,
and you try to forgive yourself for that too
now embattled land-strips with bulldozed houses
are finally harmless of access. You wish.

Northumberland Avenue

On a visit to fortress London too
you drifted away from Trafalgar Square
far as Northumberland Avenue—
its spidery branches beginning to thicken
and bud against stone façades
with row upon row of smut-coated windows
forming a fine faint grey.

Police bollards and crush barricades
cordoned the street from a protest procession,
its freedom of speech a cacophony
of causes: against global warming, the wars,
the Monopoly money …

But here in Northumberland Avenue
up the pigeons flew
through clumps of tourists, sun-showers and sun
diffused by wind-riven clouds;
here in an absence of cars,
in that week when they were to save the world,
no, banks … so we'd been told,
drifting, not far from an endless crowd's
rainbow banners, you really
could hear yourself think; you could pause
in the riverine light of a mid-afternoon,
and speak freely.

28 March 2009

Tulip Mania

'I seem to be a petty usurer in a world
manipulated largely by big usurers.'
        T. S. Eliot

1

Weather's conspiring, what do you know,
to let the surface water dry.
Muddy footprints stiffen and crack.
Lilac, iris are like a kept promise.
Those random vandals who had gone
and done harm to our gatepost
evaporate like a lost cry.

2

A drunk girl's tottering song in the street
amongst huddled couples goes by,
and, look, surviving violets
start from junk-strewn beds—
an all's-well-that-ends-well fleck in each eye.

3

Lilac and iris are like a kept promise.
Other bulbs stay underground,
protection for investments,
tubers, dried, being ready to shoot
up and down in price
with futures, tulip-, or the stock-manias.

4

Muddy footprints stiffen and crack.
Into the weather with fingers crossed,
recapitalizing perforce,
they have to dupe the likes of us
with their last rights issues … or worse.

5

You knew it! That lichen-foxed brickwork
has mortar flaking off it,
and back to partial disillusion
in the pink begonias,
I'm left to take my profit
with its losses, take them as I must—
their big idea in dissolution,
a drunk girl's tottering song in the street
or sort of self-disgust.

A New Deal

for Simon Dentith

But then a mulch of shrivelled leaves
corroborates the gloaming green
and polychrome, mock-gothic brickwork
of a knock-down home.
                              Yes, as if a crime scene,
this after-work light, dog tiredness,
and truck tracks through the lakeside mud
look like evidence, sign or clue.

Geese stand their ground and hiss at us
here, where nature reserves
its last-but-not-least, as I suppose
from an audit culture's redacted facts
we foul our nests, are overseen,
and know not what we do.

Yet it's only as much as life deserves,
this aggressive-defensive contempt of us.
Head down, eyes fixed on tracks,
I wonder at goose squadrons
that nuzzle in rain-sodden grass …
'He's composing verses for the rhododendrons!'

No; but it's not a bad guess.

Boyle Family Album

Time was, face set forward, mooching
with peripatetic stoop, your eyes
drooped too, from shyness or fear.
They were taking the literal texture
as threats made approaches, fast in a dusk.
I crossed to avoid them, gaze fixed on
the flagstones speckled with drizzle,
or black flakes of what was a burning *Sun*

(as if they hadn't a point of view ...)

but shifted now through ninety degrees,
heaved up onto a gallery wall,
with you there, raised eyes contemplating
scent-less tarmac, untouchable signs
from a childhood studying pavements,
impacted dreck in these non-places
comes back as choked off nostalgia, an anguish
at smashed tiles, gutter grates, tramlines
flush with the fibre-glass cobbles—

us caught in their painstaking slices of fate.

True Blank

'no way in which … the understanding
of life can get ahead of life itself.'
Bernard Williams

1

The world outside had lost its story.
A wintry grey-ness covered all.
As if the drear was a lack of fiction,
some were staring into screens
for menus, for alternative
likely stories they could live
the blank hours and no-places by.
Painfully early, it was Easter—
an Easter without resurrection
of greenery or sky.

2

The world outside had lost its story.
Hanging over shrubberies
or what had flashed off diamond brickwork,
plastic-bag ghosts caught on trees
flapped inside quotation marks;
but words between us, like a self-styled
understanding, a projection,
found you able to re-found
the look of things on a lack of fiction,
being reconciled.

A Period Sky

for Peter Carpenter

1

Today the sky has a period flavour,
distances whipped in by cumulus piles
covering ranges of blue
from a near turquoise through to deep azure.
Anachronistic vapour trails
intersperse grey-bellied cloud-heaps;
they rise above chimney brick, half-timbered gable,
a pink tinge on every ply.

2

Enough to make weak eyes water, the sky
bares a memory of pain
to which your heart goes out ...
Sharp on the tongue, and getting keener,
it's tickled by a kitchen garden's
fennel, thyme, rosemary, lemon verbena.

3

As if we could still hear the shrieks and far cries
worked by a Topcliffe or Ketch,
I'm wincing at the thought of it,
that torture, while gone on above it,
clouds in all their gory detail,
their glory continue to trail
at dusk ... oh empty, indifferent sky!

Easter Parades

for Isabel Vila-Vera

Thursday Night

It's a death march for the Saviour
bringing drum-thump, blared trumpet,
eye-slit hood and, don't forget,
the packed crowd's rapt behaviour.

Cross part raised, this thorn-crowned
body, while daubed wounds bleed,
reaches the church door accompanied
by a Flagellation and Glory band.

Now cameras flash, a staggering load
emerges and blood-red petals
come showering onto black candles
in a death march for the Lord.

Sunday Noon

Here comes a gold-crowned Virgin,
her float of white lilies and candles;
and so the hallelujah bundles
flung out from balconies begin.

Their shadows flick over the horde
of raised faces, on sunlit façades,
becoming a trampled ticker-tape parade's
litter for Jesus, the risen Lord.

Moments Later

Then as if for an end to atrocities,
un-forgiven, seventy years back,
the firecrackers in a salvo
air burst with flashes and smoke;

and, at that report, a white flock,
pigeons flee up to a palm bough
in Elche's Moorish public park
(as if for an end to atrocities).

2 May 2009

Rhyparographia

Like when you go into a room
but can't remember why you came,
or what for in the press of things
and, not yourself, they're there
lain on the circular table
like a Petri dish in its cone of light.
Then they start as if to life
under your abstracted stare—

two paper clips, a napkin, the remote …

and there among the odds and ends,
here it is: your scribbled note
left however long ago
with an acronym and 'Text me!'
And here you are, in a cone of lamplight,
a statue niched in its window bay,
staring at that *aide mémoire*
you forgot you wrote.

Doctrines of Unripe Times

1

A Friday, the weekend starting early,
two people sat outside a pub—
I ask them for directions,
but they're sorry, they haven't the faintest idea.
Only it's just around the corner,
this London park with its pushchair paths,
tame swans on the mirrored clouds,
its scrawny, fearless pigeons
feeding from a spilt waste bin.
Here, lake water's regarded through trees
stationed beyond a wrought-iron fence,
boughs bending under the weight they bear.

2

Apples hang down low enough
for a coot to peck at them ...

3

But into our summer, even getting what you want,
beyond row-boats and pedalos
gulls pose like a fluttering celebrity;
in punts or manoeuvred sculls
there's ambition for it, see,
as one pulls ahead, one pulls from the race,
you'll get what you're given and lump it
or not, among the world's false subtleties;
and it's all I can do to look at them,
literally, hanging down low from each bough—
green apples on the apple trees.

Rückenfiguren

'Melville, as he always does, began to reason of
Providence and futurity, and of everything that lies
beyond human ken, and informed me that he had
"pretty much made up his mind to be annihilated."'
Nathaniel Hawthorne

Ventnor

Come to life, life in this ozoned air,
back-turned figures stare
at goose waves whitening to the shoreline.
By rip-rap rocks, below an esplanade,
sea shadows their lives as autumn sunlight
shafts through clouds made
luminous along this dark horizon.
Container ships, with decks stacked high,
punctuate a slow release
of beach, waves, sky
and palaver, palaver of seabirds
as a yachtsman labours
drowns out their hurled words.

Compton Bay

The kids build castle sea defences.
At low tide, viridian
seaweed's smeared across red sandstone
rocks; day's stragglers, their eyes
turned towards an island sunset
are black marks on this cliff-edged strand.
Rückenfiguren, like demagogues,
have out what lies beyond; as one,
accepting of oblivion,

finds breakers annihilate fort defences,
the sea, in all its thoughtlessness,
it cuts them down to size.

Bonchurch

Then they thread a coastal path
by wave revetment, chine, chalk headland
through a shower's aftermath
and past the undercliff's niched home
in that forsaken graveyard, find
his unvisited tomb …

Available Light

That needing to be near the sea
as suds from surf raced up a beach,
I heard the breakers' undertone
and scrape of red stone
surface pebbles.

Maritime light glanced off glazed water
as if to give the sky a shine
through wind's assault and battery
on silhouettes in Shippard's Chine;
but when you caught me,

you caught the one continuous roar
of whitened waves into a cove
where at the cliff erosion
fossil proof's exposed
and truth is, love,

because you said it's never boring
staring out to sea
the day the clocks went forward,
truth is, it wouldn't fail,
it would prevail,

this still confounding endlessness …

The Bird-Ghost

Like winter breath on a pane of glass
sprayed with fixing medium,
like a burglar's greasy handprint
or white ectoplasm trace,
that bird of prey had hammered hard
against the built environment.

You could pick out its bent beak's blunted face
and from a slow-motion film,
the flicker of that wing feather stain.
A smudged bird, arrested in headlong attack,
its output of energy equal to its impact
on the unseen or unforeseen
(our bedroom window pane),
it had made such a stunning mark.

The Folly

Following a line of Bredon Hill
with Malverns so much cloud beyond,
our guide, she'd no idea
who had written that one ...

Her mother, once an English teacher,
she'd loved poetry;
but something put the daughter off it,
our guide appeared to say.

And she told us how this cold's
a lazy wind that blows
right through you in the Cotswolds;

it can't be bothered going round you,
come here from the Urals
with nothing in its way.

We'd been waiting by that folly
for the others to descend,
exposed, our insignificance threatened.

Absentees had bought up all
we could survey, as she went on,
a deathly wealth, the stone
dead, rust oozing from a wall ...

Purple bastard toadflax, our
guide said, and Lord Coventry's desires
were realized for a bet, that tower
raised to light his beacon fires—

she told me, seeing round both those shires.

Trouble Knows

'the old paths trouble knows'
Roy Fisher

Speckle-headed pigeons line
canal-side railings with their shit
as on a row of portaloos.

That rustling from ground cover
will be pheasants, and a duck's
splash comes through the willows.

Here, old paths trouble knows
cut through under rail tracks
by a cindered, barge-horse towpath

where gardens sloping to the water
hint how contentment settles
beyond its sluice and locks.

But a stopped heart of summer
calls on hardly touched
deposits, assets of sorrow;

and though oblique, declining sun
towards dusk some way off
seeds stubble fields with shadow

or clouds' pink-tinged, bruised greys
are trying to make light of it,
this is why you see them so.

Epigrams of Summer

Two coots have built their nest
on a tipped-over shopping trolley;
a mattress of wet plastic litter
supports twigs they've meshed together.

While mother coot is sitting pretty
in shallows and her found-art splendour,
me, I find a theme from whatever
happens to be happening …

*

Bedraggled summer, overblown,
comes at us from under trees,
their thick-surging leafage
near the season's full opacity.

So you see this opaque world,
(the piled clouds once more making
a three-dimensional sky)
it carries us on broad shoulders.

*

Back into that world once known
are glints of copper pipe-work,
fuss and palaver in pointed brick,
privet hedges, you alone.

Then a piffling kerfuffle of weather
might blear the window pane
with your memories of judgment,
of being judged again.

*

Sensitive to the initial conditions,
here I am back in a Britain
like memories of things written,
white roots under turned stones;

and I'm living a broken series
of acronyms, new-to-me terms,
rain scents, words or idioms—
things to get done beyond these.

*

It's like we've got to do to others
what had been done to me
and there's no help in it, you say,
for that misery—

as if I could be both quick and dead
by the lapping lake water, a
world once known, bankrupted,
etcetera, etcetera …

*

Cow-parsley, buttercups, seed-heads
in extents of moving waves
are traipsed past by late revellers,
house-back shadows like a stain.

Late revellers in their dribs-and-drabs
come murmuring out of the dawn.
Overcast, a world's before them,
and what to make of their lives.

*

It's a Sunday, long before car noise,
and youth's in this June daylight:
one carries a girlfriend on his back;
others stalk with naked feet

from summers gone, at other dawns,
cloudless skies, bird choruses,
a yard's tree shadow thrown against
its house-back like a stain.

*

Then a revving stationary car,
an artic's reversing *son et lumière*
and neighbour's power saw
start silence at the heart of noise.

An answering quiet in me
finds words for inaudible futures,
references this hot afternoon
and pendant red bells of fuchsias.

*

Momentary, come bungalows,
anemone-filled gardens, and enemy
infiltrations—
as if these were the front line …

Far fields are flecked with poppies:
it's like a mute complaint
about the further sacrifices
is this compliant scene!

*

Projections of irrational fears
on cornered and desperate men
are summoned by the summer's losses,
a village's mourning routine—

like an attack on the everyday
at Hungerford or Dunblane,
Whitehaven now, us implicated
in lives not being enough again.

*

From traffic by Christ's Pieces
pasts' traces can be caught
in heart-rate, chest and gut,
lawns where we tried goodbyes …

Reflected in the river's flow
now other pairs are drifting past
under a guestroom window
towards this Bridge of Sighs.

*

Naturally making a meal of these
coincidences, off the grass,
just look, beyond mock-gothic brick,
students leave accommodation

not for an unwritten land
but this one with expenses scandals,
moral lies, and *in flagrante* …
That's where they've to go on.

*

Couples lounge across the park
with cold cuts and champagne;
Polish mothers by its lake
are talking while their toddlers

take steps towards silver birch bark;
prophylactic black umbrella
rolled up, for a walking stick,
I am some antique.

*

Great flocks of migrant geese
have paused to pick at grass
like golf officials for a ball.
The mothers feed them breadcrumbs.

Beaks crowd round the toddlers.
Their shrieks fade towards a sky
from whence the geese had come
as if to entertain us all.

*

Invisible beyond a taxi windscreen,
pasts blank you on the High Street
like none of it had ever been.
Beyond this weariness and fret,

even water birds foul the new
path beside one trouble knows,
that other life to be retrieved
under the leaves of summer.

*

Still here, I walk back under leaves
past black wrought-iron gates,
over flagstones sunk in grass
and more checkered shades.

Through the event-filled ordinary
postponements of that life,
these ghosts, you might suppose,
had our pasts in sole possession.

*

Like an attack on the everyday
or kind of self-betrayal,
how could they not spoil
this summer's full array

now I've come the extra mile
to exorcise those years,
a dazzle of sunlight appears
and words, words to say?

*

In different rooms across town
our pasts had shifted course,
but their ghosts on that horizon
(it's understood between us)

are dazzled by the mote-streams
as currents of talk behind backs
come clear in a later air
and lift those words away.

Lawrie Park Avenue

by Camille Pissarro, 1871

Wisps of white cloud in a pale turquoise sky
Pissarro painted out-of-doors,
and a church spire, its creamy stone,
two or three passers-by.

He painted out one female figure.
Her pentimenti could be seen
still on the gravel, advancing towards me,
as a darker stain.

Sydenham in an early springtime
just over a century after,
not far from the hospice where she worked,
I could imagine finding us
on that avenue again.

Then here as warmth has come, at least,
there are things to do with the past—
like droplets on those steady leaves,
her Solomon's seal after rain.

And down by more leafage-filled gardens,
the flimsy petal, purple-hearted poppies
bring home illusions of another life's
occluded possibilities.

With foxglove, iris, the night-scented stock,
everything that didn't happen,
disappointed, went awry
is back as if making a mockery
of how it was, or why.

But lacking such things to do with the past,
like this figure he had painted out
who fills the air with an indelible stain,
there'd be no possibilities.

They thicken into leaf, his flanking trees.

Look, now, it's as plain as plain.

Wood Notes

Shadows extend on pine-needle beds,
across the undergrowth ferns—
as if long life's decrepitudes
had stalked us through the woods.

A beech tree trunk bore scars of old loves.
You saw sun patches in the high leaves
and felt birch-bark striations.

It was like standing by a family tree
to get back with your sense of touch
stuff mislaid down the years.

I remembered Linnaean classifications,
wood-notes you were straining to hear
or the words four parents said
and caught us unawares …

Its coppice paths were seed-strewn then.
A bird's nest on an upper bough
drew eyes from family, still un-forgiven;
but none of that mattered now.

NOTES

Westwood Dusk: The Crest Theater is a cinema at 1262 South Westwood Blvd, Los Angeles, where Hollywood movies are sometimes premiered. *Stranger than Fiction,* in which the central character discovers that his life is being written by an English novelist, was showing there in late November 2006. I had not seen the film before completing the poem. So, as Raymond Queneau might have put it, 'Les personnages de cette poésie étant réels, toute resemblance avec des individus imaginaires serait fortuite.'

At the Institute: An exhibition of Charles Sheeler's works was held at the Art Institute of Chicago between 7 October 2006 and 7 January 2007. See Charles Brock, *Charles Sheeler: Across Media* (National Gallery of Art, Washington, and University of California Press, 2006).

Enigma Variations: Rembrandt van Rijn was born on 15 July 1606. *The Night Watch* is in the Rijksmuseum, Amsterdam, his *Bathsheba* in the Louvre.

South Shore Line: This private railroad runs around the south shore of Lake Michigan, from Randolph, Chicago, to South Bend, Indiana. The titles of the five sections are among its stations.

Peripheral Visions: The poem is set in a northern suburb of Parma, Italy.

Huntley & Palmers: The Reading-based biscuit-making company was founded in 1828 and had its factory between the Kennet and the Thames from 1841 to 1976. It was a first sight of their preserved office building that prompted the poem, which recalled the crumbling biscuit image in my '472 Claremont Road', *This Other Life* (Carcanet Press, 1988) and *Selected Poems 1976–2001* (Carcanet Press, 2003).

Whiteknights Park: What is now the campus of the University of Reading once formed the park of White Knights House, where Alexander Pope was introduced to the Blount sisters in 1707. Between 1798 and 1819 the park was the scene of extravagant parties hosted by the Fifth Duke of Marlborough. The original house was torn down in 1840 by, it is said, angry creditors.

165 King's Road: On 7 and 9 November 1874 an announcement appeared in *The Times* stating that 'A PARISIAN (20), of high literary and linguistic attainments, excellent conversation, will be glad to ACCOMPANY a GENTLEMAN (artists preferred), or a family wishing to travel in southern or in eastern countries. Good references. — A. R., No. 165, King's-road, Reading.'

Pension Scheme: Siobhan Kilfeather (1957–2007) was a distinguished scholar of Irish literature who died just before the publication of the final book in the Harry Potter series. Those entering the British university pension scheme in later career have the right to buy back a percentage of lost years, if they can afford it.

Graffiti Service: I'm being gently mocked with a quotation from one of my own early poems, 'The Interrupted Views': 'I come / back to the ash heaps, / the car dumps, /each graffito / taken as a welcome' and with an eye perhaps on the concluding two lines: 'Mute welcomes proliferate' and 'Home is the view I appropriate' in *Overdrawn Account* (Many Press, 1980) and *Selected Poems 1976–2001*.

Personal Credit: The epigraph is from act 2, scene 4. Hearing from Cesario (Viola disguised as a young man) about an imaginary sister invented to express her own feelings for the Duke, Orsino asks 'And what's her history?' to which Viola replies 'a blank, my lord'.

Ode to Debt: The poem was written in September 2007, after the failure of Northern Rock but before the so-called Credit Crunch of October 2008.

Double Portrait: Frans Hals painted his informal 'Marriage Portrait of Isaac Massa and Beatrix van der Laen' ca. 1622. It usually hangs in the Rijksmuseum, Amsterdam, but was on loan to the National Gallery, London, for an exhibition of Dutch portraiture in the summer of 2007.

A Little Exercise: The epigraphs are from Lewis Carroll's two Alice books. The poem's action takes place in Christchurch water meadows, Oxford.

Cemetery Junction: Luigi Meneghello (1922–2007), the Italian writer and translator, came to Reading in 1947 and later founded the Department of Italian Studies at the University, from which he retired in 1980. His memoir, *La materia di Reading*, was first published in 1997.

Graveyard Life: This poem is also set among the stones at Cemetery Junction. The epigraph is from the Preface to George Borrow's *Lavarengo* (1851).

Clear as Daylight: The epigraph cites the last three lines of 'After Reading *Children of Albion* (1969)' in Geoffrey Hill, *A Treatise of Civil Power* (Penguin Books, 2007), p. 23, which in its turn alludes to John

James, 'Bathampton Morrismen at the Rose & Crown', *Children of Albion: Poetry of the 'Underground' in Britain* ed. Michael Horowitz (Penguin Books, 1969), pp. 160–1.

Owning the Problem: I quote from no. 43 of Bradley's posthumously published *Aphorisms* (1930).

Reading Gaol: 'House Decoration' is an 1882 lecture first given in America some thirteen years before Wilde was sentenced to twenty-four months of hard labour in Reading Gaol.

Ekphrastic Marriage: The first part was written as an epithalamium for the civil partnership celebration of the visual artist Andrew McDonald and the literary scholar Peter Swaab. It was read during the official ceremony at Hackney Town Hall on 19 July 2008 and the celebration at Hoveton House, Norfolk, on 2 August. The second part was prompted by circumstantial occurrences at the second of these occasions.

Costume Drama: West Wycombe Park, Buckinghamshire, was being used as the set for the filming of a BBC *Little Dorrit* in July 2008 when the visit took place that started this poem. It is also the set for a film version of *The Importance of Being Ernest* (2002), including an incident cut from the stage play in which Algernon, as Ernest, is to be taken into custody on account of his debts.

Eastern Avenue: The epigraph is from line 9 of the first section to Tennyson's *Maud* (1855). My poem was begun at the time of the global financial crisis in October 2008.

Unearned Visuals: The poem was written as a tribute to the poet Roy Fisher on the occasion of his 80th birthday in June 2010. I am grateful to Adam Sowan for two local historical details.

Otterspool Prom: Otterspool Promenade runs along the Liverpool bank of the Mersey from Aigurth to Cressington Park. The epigraph and poem's closing phrase are from Hamlet's soliloquy at the close of Act 1, scene v.

Gasometers: The epigraph, from the final lines of Roussel's 1904 poem, reads: 'The lively and latent memory of a summer / Already dead, already far from me …'.

The Visitant: The epigraph reads '"Are you an angel?" asked a child. "I wish I were," Mignon replied.'

Fence Palings: The epigraph, which reads 'There was once a paling fence …', acknowledges the inspirational prompt of Morgenstern's poem, also alluded to in my lines 9 and 10.

Abroad Thoughts: OE, for *overseas experience,* is an acronym used in Australia and New Zealand. The statue commemorating Nurse Edith Cavell, who was shot by the Germans during the Great War, is at the end of Saint Martin's Lane, just off Trafalgar Square, London.

Life in Glimpses: The visual allusion at the beginning and end of this poem is to *Hunters in the Snow* by Pieter Breughel.

Shadowy Nobodies: The epigraph is from Coleridge's 17 July 1797 letter to Robert Southey.

Northumberland Avenue: The poem was occasioned by a visit to London that happened to coincide with extensive protests in response to the concurrent economic summit of the G8 countries.

Tulip Mania: The epigraph is from T. S. Eliot, 'The Idea of a Christian Society', *Christianity and Culture* (San Diego: Harcourt, Brace Jovanovich, [1939] 1977), p. 77.

Boyle Family Album: The Boyle Family of visual artists is particularly known for low relief, hyperrealist reconstructions of pavements, gutters, and other passages of urban detritus. The stated aim of their work is to represent such textured environmental experiences without nostalgia.

True Blank: The epigraph is from Bernard Williams, 'There are many kinds of eyes', *The Sense of the Past: Essays in the History of Philosophy* ed. Myles Burnyeat (Princeton: Princeton University Press, 2006), p. 328.

A Period Sky: Richard Topcliffe (1531–1604) and Jack Ketch (died 1683) were notoriously sadistic English torturers and executioners.

Easter Parades: This poem was occasioned by a visit to Elche, near Alicante, at Easter 2009, when Spain was remembering the seventieth anniversary of the end to its Civil War. The second and third of May 1808 are the dates of the uprising and executions commemorated in Goya's paintings with those dates for their titles.

Rhyparographia: This word, which I found in Julian Bell, *What is Painting? Representation and Modern Art* (London: Thames and Hudson, 1999), means the representation of ordinary things.

Doctrines of Unripe Times: I have adopted the phrase 'the doctrine of unripe times' from the Conservative prime minister (1990–1997) John Major's use of it during a BBC interview to mean one reason why appropriate policies cannot be made into effective laws at particular moments.

Rückenfiguren: The poem's title is the term used in the discussion of paintings by Caspar David Friedrich to indicate two or more figures with their backs to the viewer. The epigraph is from the entry for 20 November 1856 in Nathaniel Hawthorne, *The English Notebooks.* The conversation took place among the sand hills at Seaforth, staring across the Mersey estuary. Against his wishes, A. C. Swinburne was given a Christian burial in the graveyard of St Boniface at Bonchurch on the Isle of Wight.

Available Light: The poem's title is a phrase used in photography to refer to pictures taken without any artificial lighting effects. It is also set on the Isle of Wight.

Trouble Knows: The title and epigraph is from the first part of 'Diversions' by Roy Fisher in *The Long and the Short of It: Poems 1955–2005* (Tarset: Bloodaxe Books, 2005), p. 305. It is also alluded to in 'Epigrams of Summer'.

The Folly: The poem takes place at Broadway Tower in the Cotswolds. The one that the guide doesn't quite recall is XXI 'Bredon Hill' by A. E. Housman in *A Shropshire Lad* (1896).

Lawrie Park Avenue: The painting by Camille Pissarro is in fact called 'The Avenue, Sydenham', the name for Lawrie Park Avenue in 1871. It hangs in the National Gallery, London.

Wood Notes: The poem is located at The Vyne, Hampshire, and plays, of course, on John Milton's phrase in 'L'Allegro' describing Shakespeare as warbling 'his native wood-notes wild'.

Lightning Source UK Ltd.
Milton Keynes UK
UKOW052027141211

183776UK00001B/9/P